UNOFFICIAL
GUIDES
JUNIOR

Starter Guide to
The Legend of Zelda

T0002286

by Josh Gregory

 CHERRY LAKE PRESS
Ann Arbor, Michigan

CHERRY LAKE PRESS

Published in the United States of America by Cherry Lake Publishing
Ann Arbor, Michigan
www.cherrylakepublishing.com

Reading Adviser: Beth Walker Gambro, MS, Ed., Reading Consultant, Yorkville, IL

Photo Credits: Images by Josh Gregory

Copyright © 2024 by Cherry Lake Publishing Group

Cherry Lake Press is an imprint of Cherry Lake Publishing Group.

Library of Congress Cataloging-in-Publication Data

Names: Gregory, Josh, author.
Title: Starter guide to The Legend of Zelda / by Josh Gregory.
Description: Ann Arbor, Michigan : Cherry Lake Publishing, [2024] | Series:
    Unofficial Guides Junior | Includes bibliographical references and
    index. | Audience: Grades 4-6
Identifiers: LCCN 2023043879 (print) | LCCN 2023043880 (ebook) | ISBN
    9781668937808 (hardcover) | ISBN 9781668938843 (paperback) | ISBN
    9781668940181 (epub) | ISBN 9781668941539 (pdf) | ISBN 9781668942888
    (Kindle edition) | ISBN 9781668944233 (ebook)
Subjects: LCSH: Legend of Zelda (Game)—Handbooks, manuals, etc.
Classification: LCC GV1469.35.L43 G75 2024 (print) | LCC GV1469.35.L43
    (ebook) | DDC 794.8—dc23/eng/20230925
LC record available at https://lccn.loc.gov/2023043879
LC ebook record available at https://lccn.loc.gov/2023043880

Printed in the United States of America by
Corporate Graphics

Note from the Publisher: Websites change regularly, and their future contents are outside of our control. Supervise children when conducting any recommended online searches for extended learning opportunities.

Contents

Action and Adventure!

Players enjoy finding their way through the world of *The Legend of Zelda*.

There's a video game that's packed with action and adventure. People love playing it. It's called *The Legend of Zelda*. And it's one of the most popular video game **series** of all time! Nintendo first released *The Legend of Zelda* in 1986. Today, there are many more Zelda games. Let's explore them!

Zelda's Designer

The game's designer, Shigeru Miyamoto, is from Japan. He also created *Donkey Kong* and the *Mario Brothers* series!

Game Basics

The *Legend of Zelda* follows Link on many missions.

The Legend of Zelda games center on Link, an elf-like boy. He lives in a magical country called Hyrule. The other main character is Princess Zelda. She and Link are on a mission to save Hyrule from a wicked **warlord**. His name is Ganon. To gain power, Ganon tries to take the Triforce. This special **artifact** can grant any wish.

Triforce

The Triforce is made up of three triangles. They stand for power, wisdom, and courage.

Starting Out

Link needs to gather supplies and tools to stay alive.

There are many Zelda games to play. But each one starts out the same. The character Link is waking up from a long sleep. Link may have been asleep for 100 years! So it's up to you to discover what happened during that time. Link must explore the land and regain his memories. He also needs to find supplies. These will help him and Zelda.

A Vast World

The world of Zelda is huge! Players can spend many hours playing it and not experience everything.

Which Game?

Scope

Edit pins ⊖   Quit Ⓑ   Place pin Ⓐ

The Sheikah Slate has a scope. A scope lets you see things that are far away. This scope allows you to spy on enemies.

Which Zelda game should you play? *Breath of the Wild* is a good place to start. It takes place in a big, open world. As Link wakes up, you will hear a voice. Do as it says. It will help you start your journey. The voice will also help you complete tasks. For example, it will lead you to the **shrines**. Each one contains challenges.

Sheikah Slate

Link has a tool called a Sheikah Slate. It looks like a Nintendo Switch. The slate has a map and can be used to solve puzzles.

Special Abilities

Gliding is one of the most important skills in *Breath of the Wild*.

Completing challenges at the first four shrines will give you runes. These runes grant you special abilities. For example, the Magnesis Rune lets you move metal objects. The Stasis Rune allows you to stop time. And the Cryonis Rune turns water into ice. Runes are needed to solve puzzles. You can also use them to defeat enemies and advance in the game. After unlocking the runes, the voice will give you a glider.

An Open World

A green stamina wheel will pop up anytime you start sprinting.

You'll use the glider throughout the game. It will allow you to freely explore Hyrule! Once you land, you can walk or jog. To do this on a Nintendo Switch, press the left control stick in any direction. If you hold down the B button, you can also sprint. If you move toward a wall or mountain, Link can climb it. These actions require **stamina**. Rest up to **restore** your stamina.

Different Devices

The Legend of Zelda games can be played on different devices. Each device may have different controls. Use the game's tutorial to learn the controls you need on your device.

Survival Skills

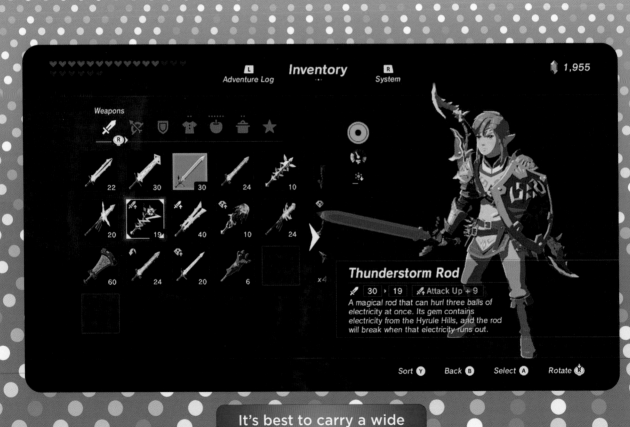

Inventory

L Adventure Log   R System

🡒 1,955

Weapons

22   30   30   24   10

20   19   40   10   24

60   24   20   6   x 4

Thunderstorm Rod

🗡 30 ▸ 19   ⚔ Attack Up + 9

A magical rod that can hurl three balls of electricity at once. Its gem contains electricity from the Hyrule Hills, and the rod will break when that electricity runs out.

Sort Y   Back B   Select A   Rotate 🕹

It's best to carry a wide range of weapons.

Hyrule can be a dangerous place. There are many enemies. How can you defend yourself? One way is to attack them with weapons. Sometimes, you'll find weapons in treasure chests or on the ground. Other times, enemies will drop them. There are also special weapons. These can only be won through quests.

Strong Weapons

Not all the weapons you find will last. Some will break after a few swings. This means you should always be on the hunt for new, stronger weapons.

More Adventure

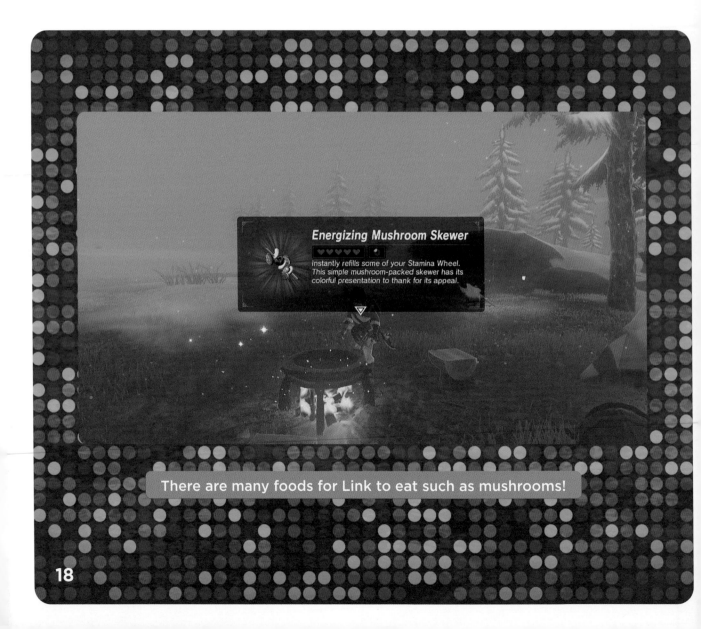

Energizing Mushroom Skewer

Instantly refills some of your Stamina Wheel. This simple mushroom-packed skewer has its colorful presentation to thank for its appeal.

There are many foods for Link to eat such as mushrooms!

Be smart about fighting. Use your rune abilities against enemies. Also, find things like boulders to roll at your enemies. If Link gets hurt, he'll need to eat to heal. If you are brave, you can head to the game's final battle. But it may be worth completing the game's other goals first.

Making Money

Money in *Breath of the Wild* is in the form of rupees. You can use rupees to buy gear and other things.

What's Next?

At the start of *Tears of the Kingdom*, the world is shown as floating islands in the sky.

In 2023, a new Zelda game was released. It's called *Tears of the Kingdom*. In it, players get to explore an even bigger world. In the game, you can create boats and cars. You can also use a magic arm to move things. No matter the series, Zelda will always bring adventure. So start exploring!

GLOSSARY

artifact (ART-uh-fakt) an object made by people

restore (ri-STOR) to bring back

series (SIHR-eez) a set of games

shrines (SHRYNZ) special places built to remember or celebrate something

stamina (STA-mih-nuh) a person or animal's ability to do something for a long time without resting

warlord (WOR-lord) a powerful military ruler

FIND OUT MORE

BOOKS

Cunningham, Kevin. *Video Game Designer*. Ann Arbor, MI: Cherry Lake Publishing, 2016.

Loh-Hagan, Virginia. *Video Games*. Ann Arbor, MI: Cherry Lake Publishing, 2021.

Powell, Marie. *Asking Questions About Video Games*. Ann Arbor, MI: Cherry Lake Publishing, 2016.

WEBSITES

With an adult, learn more online with these suggested searches:

The Legend of Zelda: Breath of the Wild
Check out the latest updates on the official *Breath of the Wild* website.

The Legend of Zelda: Breath of the Wild—Zelda Wiki
Check out this fan-created guide when you need really detailed Zelda information.

The Legend of Zelda: Tears of the Kingdom
Learn about the newest game in the series.

INDEX

ABOUT THE AUTHOR

Josh Gregory is the author of more than 200 books for kids. He has written about everything from animals to technology to history. A graduate of the University of Missouri–Columbia, he currently lives in Chicago, Illinois.